JOEL OSTEEN

Author of 10 *New York Times* Bestsellers

peaceful

on

purpose

STUDY GUIDE

The Power to Remain Calm, Strong and Confident in Every Season

Faith
Words

New York • Nashville

peaceful

on

purpose

STUDY GUIDE

Also by Joel Osteen

Contents

Introduction

We are delighted that you have chosen to use this study guide that was written as a companion to *Peaceful on Purpose*. Every day you have opportunities to get upset, to be offended, and to live worried. People say and do things that get on your nerves. Unexpected bills and setbacks come. The medical report is not good. The problem is that if we lose our peace because someone did us wrong or life throws us a curve, we allow our circumstances to determine whether or not we're going to be happy. We set ourselves up for a lifetime of disappointments when we expect all our plans to work out the way we want and other people to treat us right. God never promised that He would keep us from difficulties. But He did say that He has given us the power to remain calm in times of adversity.

You may have many reasons for why you get discouraged, fearful, anxious, and not able to sleep at night, but it's not okay to let those feelings stay. You have the strength you need to guard your heart and mind and keep what's outside from getting inside. God says to be still and know that He is God. When you live in this place of faith and trust, this place of peace, you're in a position of power. You have already made up your mind to stay in peace, knowing God will work out His plans for your life.

The thoughts and questions addressed in this study guide will help you learn to live in peace, to stay positive, hopeful, and at rest. You will be encouraged to stand strong and not be moved by your circumstances, by negative comments, or by critics. You will discover the way to the peace that surpasses understanding.

This study has been created so that it lends itself to self-study or personal development as well as small-group study or discussion, say in a care group or book club setting. Whichever the purpose you have in mind, you'll find great opportunity to personally be blessed as you take time to study and meditate on God's Word.

The format of each chapter is simple and user-friendly. For maximum benefit, it is best to first read the corresponding chapter from *Peaceful on Purpose*, and then work your way through the chapter in this study guide. The majority of the questions are personal, and taking the time to read through the chapters in the book and think through how each question can affect your life will give the study immediate personal application.

If you decide to use this study guide in a small group study, the most effective way is to go through each chapter on your own as preparation before each meeting. Take some time to read the relevant portions of text and to reflect on the questions and how they apply to you. This will give your group study depth and make the sessions more productive for all.

Because of the personal nature of this study, if you use it in a group setting or on a retreat, remember that confidentiality, courtesy, and mutual respect lay the foundation for a healthy group. A small group should be a safe place for all who participate. Don't let your conversations leave the small group. A small group is not a place to tell others what they should have done or said or think, and it's not a place to force opinions on others. Commit yourselves to listening in love to one another, to praying for and supporting one another, to being sensitive to their perspectives, and to showing each participant the grace you would like to receive from others.

• • •

CHAPTER ONE

All Is Well

It's easy to go through life worried about the future, frustrated because a dream is taking so long to come to pass, upset because somebody did you wrong. But instead of complaining about the difficulty, instead of being upset because your plans didn't work out, instead of losing your peace, you need to remember this simple phrase: *All is well.* God is still on the throne. He's directing your steps. He wouldn't have allowed it unless He had a purpose. When you're tempted to get discouraged, keep reminding yourself that all is well.

1. As you consider the discouragements you are facing, what is your immediate response to having the attitude that *all is well*? Describe your typical attitude in response to difficulties.

....

....

....

....

....

....

2. What difference does having an "all is well" attitude make?

....

....

....

....

....

....

You have a made-up mind. You know God is bigger than anything you're facing.

3. Read Daniel 3. What difficulty confronted the three Hebrew teenagers? Describe their attitude when faced with what looked like instantaneous death. What happened as a result?

....

....

....

....

....

....

....

....

4. Had you been with Shadrach, Meshach, and Abednego, how do you see yourself responding?

....

....

....

....

....

....

5. Describe one situation you are facing now that you don't see an answer to or a way out. What change in your thinking will help you start to turn this around?

....

....

....

....

....

....

What's interesting is that the Hebrew teenagers were doing the right thing when the wrong thing happened to them. Being in God's perfect will doesn't mean you won't have difficulties. You can't reach your destiny without opposition, unfair situations, and people doing you wrong.

6. What does 1 Peter 4:12 tell you to do when life throws you a curve?

....

....

....

....

7. Read Matthew 13:24–29. What are the weeds in your life, and where do they come from? What are the weeds a sign of?

....

....

....

....

....

....

....

....

> *Anytime you're doing the right thing, don't be surprised if you find weeds springing up.*

8. When you see a difficulty springing up, instead of losing your peace and falling apart with discouragement, what should you tell yourself?

....

....

....

....

....

....

9. The Parable of the Wheat and Weeds ends with the farmer telling his workers to not pull up the weeds. What is God saying to us about the weeds?

....

....

....

....

10. The Scripture says, "For only we who believe God can enter into his place of rest" (Heb. 4:3 TLB). What does this tell you about trying to fix your struggles and difficulties?

....

....

....

....

....

....

Too often we get frustrated by difficulties, but you have to realize you can't have a harvest without a few weeds.

11. Describe the weeds in David's life and Joseph's life. Where would they not have gotten to without those weeds? What do you see as the biggest weeds in your life?

....

....

....

....

....

....

....

12. What lesson can you take from the couple who were finalizing the contract on their first house when the husband lost his job? How did their attitude make a difference in how they handled this challenge?

....

....

....

....

....

13. Read 2 Kings 4:8–37. Facing the tragic death of her son, how did this mother show the type of faith that "calls those things which do not exist as though they did" (Rom. 4:17 NKJV)? What was God showing us about using our words to change situations?

....

....

....

....

....

....

14. You may have a situation today that is not well. Rather than accepting it and getting discouraged, write a statement of faith that declares you dare to believe that "all is well."

....

....

....

....

....

15. Read Acts 16:16–34. Describe Paul and Silas's situation in Philippi and how their response turned it around with an amazing result.

....

....

....

....

....

....

Job went through a season of great trouble, losing his health, his business, and his children. But he didn't get bitter. Instead, he said, "Though He slay me, yet will I trust Him" (Job 13:15 NKJV).

16. What was Job meaning in that declaration? Write a statement that reflects a mature attitude that will keep you from being moved by your circumstances and that takes the power of the enemy away.

> *If you're only going to be happy if everything happens your way, you're setting yourself up for disappointment.*

....

....

....

....

....

....

17. How did Daniel represent the power of "all is well" when he faced the lions' den?

....

....

....

....

18. Write out the words that Horatio Spafford wrote as he grieved the loss of his four daughters. What is its message of hope for you today and for the future?

....

....

....

....

....

....

....

....

....

19. When things in your life seem out of control, why do you need to announce that "all is well" so the enemy can hear it?

....

....

....

....

....

....

20. How you respond in the difficult times will determine whether or not you make it into the fullness of your destiny. Write out some specific ways that is shown as true.

....

....

....

....

....

....

....

....

You may be in a situation where you could easily be worried, upset, and give up on your dreams. You don't see how it can turn around. The prophet Isaiah says, "Say to the righteous that it shall be well with them" (Isa. 3:10 NKJV). You are the righteous. God is saying this to you: "It shall be well with you." Not maybe, not I hope so, not if you get lucky—no, God promises it shall be well.

21. What is God saying to you about your troubling situation?

> *You may be saying it by faith today, but as the mother did with Elisha, one day you will say "All is well" as a fact.*

....

....

....

....

....

....

....

....

....

....

22. Write a prayer to the Lord, telling Him how you feel as you reflect on what you have learned in this chapter.

....

....

....

....

....

....

....

....

· · ·

CHAPTER TWO

Protect Your Peace

We should get up every morning believing for a good day, expecting favor, knowing that God is directing our steps. At the same time, we should realize that everything may not go perfectly. Every person may not treat us right. Our plans may not stay on schedule. There may be some bumps in the road, things that we didn't see coming.

1. Just as you carry a spare tire in your car in case one of the tires goes flat, you need to make provision every day in case things don't go your way. What are some of the things that come against you every day that try to steal your peace? How can you make sure you have your spare tire in place to stay in peace?

    ....

    ....

    ....

    ....

    ....

    ....

    ....

2. If you are going to stay in peace with imperfect people, what do you need to realize about them, and how do you need to be prepared to respond to them?

    ....

    ....

    ....

    ....

    ....

Here's a key to protecting your peace: Your happiness is not someone else's responsibility. You are responsible for your own happiness.

3. What happens when you start counting on other people to keep you feeling good? Describe a time when you looked to someone else to give you what only God can give. What was the result?

....

....

....

....

....

....

4. Name an area of your life that is like a pothole you keep hitting that keeps you upset and discouraged. Write down the words of truth that will help keep you moving forward.

....

....

....

....

....

....

5. How does going around offended and upset dishonor God? What is the way to honor Him and move past what keeps you stuck?

....

....

....

....

....

....

The Scripture says God has given "him power to keep himself calm in the days of adversity" (Ps. 94:13 AMPC). You don't have to let the same things keep upsetting you. Quit telling yourself, "I can't help it. They just know how to push my buttons." Try a new approach. Decide ahead of time that you're going to stay in peace, and you'll tap into that power to remain calm.

6. As with the man who bought the newspaper in the store, there may be people you see every day who have the gift of getting on your nerves. How do you respond to them? What change in your thinking will help you improve in this area?

Don't go the next thirty years letting the same things upset you, giving away your power.

....

....

....

....

....

....

....

....

7. How do you respond when you encounter someone who is condescending and rude? What should you keep in mind about them? What will happen if you rise above their criticism?

....

....

....

....

....

....

....

....

It's easy to let another person ruin your day. It's easy to let a grouchy boss make you grouchy, and then you take it home with you and are sour with your family. You can't keep it from happening, but you can keep it from getting inside. You have to guard your heart.

8. Jesus says, "For offenses will inevitably come" (Matt. 18:7 CSB). How should you prepare to handle negative comments from other people?

....

....

....

....

....

9. Where does the word *offenses* come from? Describe the enemy's strategy against you.

....

....

....

....

....

....

....

10. What areas do you find yourself most vulnerable to being baited into conflict? What truths do you need to tell yourself to protect your peace?

....

....

....

....

....

....

....

Are you fighting battles that don't matter that are also keeping you from battles that do matter? You have to learn to walk away from petty arguments, from disrespect, and from jealous people. "Avoiding a fight is a mark of honor" (Prov. 20:3 NLT). Walking away from a fight is not being weak; that takes a strong person. That's a mark of honor.

11. When David heard Goliath taunting the Israelite army, he faced two battles. What were they, and which one did he walk away from? Why was this such a wise choice?

....

....

....

....

....

....

....

12. In a relationship, such as being married, the Scripture says one can chase a thousand, and two can put ten thousand to flight (see Deut. 32:30). How can you maintain your unity and be at peace with each other as you face your battles together?

....

....

....

....

....

13. Write out Psalm 141:3 and take some time to memorize this powerful biblical principle. If you make this your prayer, how will it help you defeat giants?

....

....

....

....

14. When you hear negative, false things being said about you, when people are trying to discredit you, it's tempting to respond. Read Psalm 23:5. What powerful truth is reflected in David's words that will help you respond to someone who is coming against you?

....

....

....

....

....

....

....

15. What kinds of opposition did the apostle Paul face? What can you learn from his statement in 2 Timothy 4:14–15?

....

....

....

....

....

....

16. What situations in your life are you fighting when you should be sitting? Take some time to reflect on it and write an honest review.

....

....

....

....

....

....

....

17. Read 1 Samuel 10:17–27 NLT. Why did a small group of people make fun of Saul? What valuable lesson can you take from his response to them?

....

....

....

....

....

....

....

18. Read Nehemiah 4:1–15. What actions did Sanballat and Tobiah take against Nehemiah and the rebuilding of the walls of Jerusalem? How did Nehemiah respond?

....

....

....

....

....

....

....

19. Name a dream or desire of your heart that has come under ridicule and criticism. How did you respond, and what was the outcome?

....

....

....

....

....

....

There will always be people who try to get you riled up. Don't let them steal your peace.

20. Read Ephesians 6:10–17. It's interesting that the one piece of the armor God chose for peace is our shoes. What does that tell you about the other pieces of the armor, and why is it so important to make sure you put on your shoes of peace?

....

....

....

....

....

....

....

....

....

....

21. What does peace have to do with power? Have you recognized this is true in your life? In what ways do you, and in what ways have you not? What change in your thinking will help you improve in this area?

....

....

....

....

....

....

....

....

....

....

....

....

. . .

CHAPTER THREE

The Guardian of Your Soul

When we watch the news and see natural disasters, accidents, conflicts between nations, and pandemics, it's easy to live worried and afraid. All these concerns are valid. If you were on your own, you would have a reason to lose your peace and be worried. But the Scripture says, "You have turned to your Shepherd, the Guardian of your souls" (1 Pet. 2:25 NLT). You are not in this by yourself. You have a protector, a defender, a deliverer.

1. Read Psalm 91. Write down God's promises of protection that are found in this psalm.

    ....
    ....
    ....
    ....
    ....
    ....
    ....

2. Because you turned to your Shepherd, write out some of the specific ways that you feel He's protected you from things you knew nothing about.

    You can't go anywhere without your Guardian God.

    ....
    ....
    ....
    ....
    ....

3. Read Psalm 121. What is its message of hope for you today and for the future?

....

....

....

....

....

....

....

4. Read Exodus 9:1–7. Describe the remarkable thing that God did repeatedly when He sent plagues upon Pharaoh and the Egyptian people.

....

....

....

....

....

....

5. In what ways have you recognized this same distinction in your life—that what happened to others did not happen to you?

....

....

....

....

....

....

....

6. God has a shield around your life that keeps the enemy out. What are some declarations you need to make that the enemy cannot touch you?

7. We all have difficulties. Sickness, opposition, and betrayals may come, but they don't have to stay. How is it possible to keep the door closed when they knock?

None of the difficulties belong to you. They're on foreign territory.

8. When you face a sickness, a bad break, or a loss, does that mean you don't have a distinction on you or that you don't have enough faith? What did Jesus say about it in Matthew 5:45? As you fight the good fight of faith, what assurance does this give you?

Psalm 91 NKJV opens by saying, "He who dwells in the secret place of the Most High shall abide under the shadow of the Almighty." The next verse says, "I will say of the LORD, 'He is my refuge and my fortress; my God, in Him I will trust.'"

9. Why is it significant that the psalmist didn't just say, "I'm going to stay in the secret place and that will keep me protected," but instead he says, "I will say of the LORD"?

    ....

    ....

    ....

    ....

    ....

    ....

10. What are some of the things you say regularly that you need to zip it up? What do you need to be saying if you want to activate God's protection and favor?

    ....

    ....

    ....

    ....

    ....

    ....

11. When David faced opposition, he knew how to activate this shield of protection. What comfort and assurance do you find in his words in Psalm 27?

    ....

    ....

    ....

    ....

    ....

12. Read 1 Samuel 23:1–18. Why was King Saul trying to kill David? Despite David's being at a great disadvantage, why couldn't Saul track him down?

....

....

....

....

....

13. When you're doing the right thing and people or situations are coming against you, why do you have no reason to worry?

....

....

....

....

....

14. Read 1 Samuel 23:19–29. David had no idea that local men had betrayed him and told Saul his location. Even though there was no way for David to escape, what did he continue to do? What happened at the very last moment before David would have been taken?

....

....

....

....

....

15. What does this tell you about God's ability to protect you? What is the one thing that you need to do?

....

....

....

....

16. In Matthew 24, Jesus says that in the last days there will be epidemics, earthquakes, famines, wars and rumors of war. An epidemic is a worldwide outbreak of disease like what we experienced with the coronavirus. When you feel fear and panic, what can you remind yourself to keep anchored to peace?

....

....

....

....

....

....

17. Living in a world that's like an ocean of negativity around us, what steps can you take to keep the water from coming into your boat?

A ship doesn't sink because of the water around it.

....

....

....

....

....

....

....

18. Search out and write down Scriptures that cover the areas of your need, and arm yourself with them.

....

....

....

....

....

....

We all face times of being overwhelmed by challenges, pressures, and opposition on every side. It may feel at times as though we're trapped in a war zone with bombs exploding around us and being pursued by the enemy.

19. Read Isaiah 54:17. What message of hope do you feel God is speaking to your heart about as you consider Him the Guardian of your soul? How can you apply this in your daily life?

....

....

....

....

....

....

....

....

20. Read 2 Kings 6:8–23. The Syrian king sent "horses and chariots and a great army" to capture one man, the prophet Elisha. Recount the story through the eyes of Elisha's servant. What encouragement does this give you to be confident and assured that God will display His awesome power when you feel overwhelmed?

....

....

....

....

....

....

....

....

....

The Moses sole is a small fish that swims in the same waters of the Red Sea as large sharks that typically eat these kinds of fish. However, the Moses sole has a unique defense system that naturally secretes poisonous toxins from its glands that keeps the sharks' jaws frozen in position from biting down.

21. Describe the defense system God has given you to keep the enemy from defeating you.

> *Negative talk is like bait. It attracts the enemy.*

....

....

....

....

....

....

....

....

22. After reading this chapter, how do you feel, knowing that the Most High God is the Guardian of your soul? Write a declaration that you will use to silence the voices that tell you there is no hedge of protection around you.

....

....

....

....

....

....

....

....

....

....

• • •

CHAPTER FOUR

Peace with Yourself

We all make mistakes and do things we know we shouldn't. It's easy to go around with a heaviness, feeling badly about ourselves. But living with guilt doesn't help you to do better; it causes you to struggle more. Guilt drains you emotionally. When we're guilty, we don't pursue dreams or believe we can overcome challenges. We aren't at peace. We get stuck.

1. According to Revelation 12:10, what is one of the names of the enemy? How does he work overtime to destroy your peace? What ways do you see this impacting your life today?

....

....

....

....

....

....

2. Write out 1 John 1:9 and take some time to commit it to memory. Where do you need to get in agreement with God and start believing this is true for you?

....

....

....

....

....

....

3. Read 2 Corinthians 5:21. What does *righteous* mean, and how does one become righteous?

4. The apostle Paul writes of "those who receive the abundance of grace and of the gift of righteousness" (Rom. 5:17 NKJV). When the accusing voices remind you of your failures and how you don't measure up, what do you have to declare? How do you receive God's gift?

Who are you going to believe?

5. Proverbs 28:1 NKJV says, "The righteous are bold as a lion." If you are unsure and doubtful, what will happen? Write a bold statement declaring who God has made you.

Sometimes it's as though we're carrying all these heavy bags around. Everywhere we go, they weigh us down. Before we leave the house, we pick up a bag of guilt. Then we load up another bag with everything we did wrong, but there are so many mistakes that we start to fill another bag. That bag still has some room, so we add in a long list of regrets.

6. Reflect upon the heavy bags that you are conscious of carrying right now. What impact are they having on your daily life?

....

....

....

....

....

....

....

7. Read Hebrews 12:1. It's time to lay aside those weights you have been carrying. How can you start to get rid of the baggage of guilt and shame that holds you back today?

....

....

....

....

....

....

8. What is it like to receive the gift of righteousness as a child receives a gift?

....

....

....

....

....

9. When we do something wrong, what is the difference between genuine remorse and staying down to show God that we're sorry? Why can we never pay God back for our mistakes?

    ....

    ....

    ....

    ....

    ....

10. Read Isaiah 43:25. What are the two things that God promises He does when we ask Him to forgive us? How is that even possible?

    ....

    ....

    ....

    ....

    ....

11. Is there something that you've done wrong that you keep asking God to forgive over and over? Why do you keep telling Him how bad you feel? Write a statement of faith that you are believing what He says and that you are letting it go and forgetting it as well.

> *Mercy covers our mistakes. Mercy gives you what you don't deserve.*

    ....

    ....

    ....

    ....

    ....

    ....

    ....

    ....

12. Read Jonah 1–3:1. What had Jonah done? Despite that, what did God say to him when he found himself on dry ground again? What was God showing us about Himself?

....

....

....

....

....

....

....

....

13. Do you tend to categorize your mistakes by degrees? Describe your thinking on different degrees of mistakes and how long you think you should feel bad about them. Is your thinking in alignment with what God has said?

....

....

....

....

....

....

....

14. What do you think the accuser was telling Jonah when God stepped in and told him to go to Nineveh the second time?

....

....

....

....

15. God can't use you in the way He wants when you live feeling guilty, condemned, and down on yourself. What did Jonah have to do that we all must do?

....

....

....

....

....

16. Are you letting a mistake you made or a personal failure to convince you that God can't use you now? What message of hope do you feel God is personally speaking to you?

> *You don't have to sit on the sidelines of life. Get your peace back.*

....

....

....

....

....

....

17. Write a prayer to the Lord, telling Him how you feel as you reflect on the fact that God does not give us time-outs, that He corrects us when we do wrong and says, "Move forward."

....

....

....

....

....

....

18. Read Judges 16. It was correctly predicted that Samson would do great things, but what happened along the way? How did God use Samson "one more time"?

....

....

....

....

....

....

....

19. After you have made mistakes and you feel washed-up, how do you get your passion back, your peace back? What truth will you tell yourself to get back in the game?

....

....

....

....

....

....

....

20. Read Romans 8:1–5. When you make a mistake, how will you respond if you are "in the flesh"? How will you respond if you "walk in the Spirit"? How can you start to live a life truly free from condemnation?

....

....

....

....

....

....

....

Just because you feel guilty doesn't mean you are guilty. You can't go by your feelings. Feelings don't always tell us the truth. You might not feel forgiven, but you are forgiven. You might not feel holy, and you don't perform perfectly all the time, but you are holy.

21. James 4:7 NIV says, "Resist the devil, and he will flee from you." What does *resist* mean? What accusation does the enemy use against you the most to hold you back? What promise of Scripture can you use to strengthen your heart and win the battle today?

....

....

....

....

....

....

....

....

22. You need to have an imaginary sticker on you that says "guilt-free," "condemnation-free," or "heaviness-free." What have you learned in this chapter that will enable you to walk in freedom?

When the accuser tries to dump that load of guilt on you, just show him your sticker.

....

....

....

....

....

....

....

• • •

CHAPTER FIVE

God's Got This

We all have things that come against us. It's easy to live uptight, wondering how it's going to work out. What if the medical report isn't good? What if my finances don't get better? We tried to figure it out, we've done our best, but we don't see anything changing. If we're not careful, we'll lose our peace and live worried and discouraged, not expecting it to get better.

1. What was your immediate response to the statement "God's got this"? When you face a difficult situation or have a lack in your life, is this truth about God firmly rooted in your heart? Write an honest review of what you think. What change in your thinking will help you improve in this area and stay in peace?

....

....

....

....

....

....

....

....

....

....

....

....

....

....

....

....

> *Instead of trying to force it to happen and living uptight, you have to let go and let God.*

2. Sometimes, maybe oftentimes, we're trying to play God. Reflect on some ways that you find yourself doing that. Be specific with your examples. What truth will you tell yourself to keep you from living frustrated in the future?

....

....

....

....

....

....

....

....

....

....

....

3. Read Genesis 50:20. You may have a good reason to worry about something, but what is God saying to you?

....

....

....

....

....

....

....

....

God's ways are better than our ways. God knows what's best for you. He's got this.

4. Read Daniel 6. When you give your best and excel, what should not come as a surprise to you? Have you found this true in your experience? How so?

....

....

....

....

....

....

5. When Daniel was setup by the other officials, he could have compromised and stopped praying. What valuable lesson can you take from his example?

> *God has a hedge of protection around you.*

....

....

....

....

....

....

6. How did Daniel's attitude as he faced the lions' den mirror the attitude of his Hebrew friends as they were about to be thrown into a fiery furnace? How do these align with the apostle Paul's declaration "For to me, to live is Christ and to die is gain" (Phil. 1:21 NIV)?

....

....

....

....

....

....

When the authorities threw Daniel into the lions' den, God supernaturally closed the mouths of the lions. God knows how to make you unappetizing to the enemy.

7. Why can you live worry-free from the things that the enemy sends against you?

    ....
    ....
    ....
    ....
    ....
    ....
    ....

8. Describe a time when you knew you were in a "controlled environment" even though your circumstances said otherwise.

    ....
    ....
    ....
    ....
    ....
    ....

9. The Scripture says, "Neither give place to the devil" (Eph. 4:27 KJV). How do you do that when you are being confronted by the enemy?

    ....
    ....
    ....
    ....
    ....

10. What reason does the Scripture give to explain how it was possible that Daniel came out of the lions' den without a scratch? What encouragement does this give you about your faith?

....

....

....

....

....

....

....

....

Here's the key: God doesn't deliver us from every difficulty. Most of the time, He takes us through the difficulty. Daniel's faith didn't keep him out of the lions' den, but his faith did make him lion-proof. That's what brought him out of the lions' den.

11. Describe a difficult situation in your past when you got caught up in worry and panicked rather than maintained your faith. What outcome did it lead to? How can you keep from repeating your past response?

....   *Can I tell you*

....   *that God's*

....   *got this?*

....

....

....

....

....

....

David says, "Though I walk through the valley of the shadow of death, I will fear no evil" (Ps. 23:4 NKJV). God is not just with you on the mountaintops. He's with you in the valleys when you're going through difficult things. He is concerned about what concerns you.

12. The Scripture says that a sparrow doesn't fall to the ground without God knowing about it. How do you feel, knowing that you can trust Him with what's happening in your life?

....

....

....

....

....

....

13. What powerful principle was reflected in the college orientation day story? What does it tell you about what worries and stresses you out?

....

....

....

....

....

....

14. When we worry, what do we do to our relationship with the Almighty God? How can you turn that back around?

....

....

....

....

....

15. Why did God allow David to defeat Goliath? What does that tell you about some of the battles He allows in your life?

....

....

....

....

....

....

....

16. When God brings you through difficulties, how does He use it to fuel your faith when you face other challenges?

....

....

....

....

....

....

17. According to Psalm 27, when you have enemies coming against you, what advantage do you have? If you stay in peace, what are you going to see?

....

....

....

....

....

....

....

18. What assurance and encouragement can you take from the lady who had been through a divorce and was carrying all the hurt and pain?

> *It all happened when she changed her perspective.*

....

....

....

....

....

....

....

....

19. Based upon what you have learned in this chapter, what message of hope do you feel God is personally speaking to your heart about something that is weighing you down today? Spend some time giving thanks to the Lord and share with Him how this blesses you.

....

....

....

....

....

....

....

....

....

....

....

· · ·

CHAPTER SIX

It's Already Set Up

It's easy to go through life worried about how we're going to accomplish a dream, or how we're going to get out of a problem, or how we're going to meet the right person. We look at all the reasons why it's not going to work out, but when God laid out the plan for your life, He lined up everything you need to fulfill your destiny—every good break, every person, every solution. He's not trying to figure out how to do it. Stay in peace. It's already set up.

1. How did you feel when you read the statement that God has already set up the answer to the problem you don't think will turn around? Do you believe that's true?

....

....

....

....

....

....

....

2. Read Luke 22:7–13. Describe how detailed Jesus was in making arrangements for the Passover meal that is now known as the Last Supper.

....

....

....

....

....

....

3. Every detail of the Last Supper was already set up before the disciples got there. What does that tell you about how He is directing your steps and orchestrating things around you? How does that make you feel knowing this?

> *It was the right person, the right house, and the right timing.*

4. What valuable lesson can you take from the man who went to a government office and was treated rudely by a clerk who didn't seem to like him?

5. Write out Isaiah 14:27 and begin to commit it to memory. What is God saying to you?

6. Even when you've been treated unfairly and you're disappointed about what didn't work out, what good news can you take from the story of the Compaq Center?

....

....

....

....

....

....

....

....

....

....

7. We all face something that we can't see how it's ever going to work out, how we'll get the breaks we need. What is that thing in your life, and what truth about God will keep you from being frustrated? Write a prayer of thanks to God that you are expecting His goodness.

....

....

....

....

....

....

....

....

....

....

....

....

8. Read Mark 11:1–11. What did the disciples find when they obeyed Jesus' instructions?

....

....

....

....

9. Read Zechariah 9:9, which was written well over five hundred years before this fulfill-ment. What didn't the disciples realize when they went to get the colt that day?

....

....

....

....

10. What do we need to realize as we go about our normal daily routine? What ways do you see this remarkable truth impacting your life?

Your life has been prophesied.

....

....

....

....

....

....

....

....

....

....

....

11. The colt that Jesus rode had never been ridden before. It had been kept to fulfill Zechariah's prophecy. What does this show you about what God has ordained for your life?

....

....

....

....

....

....

....

....

12. Describe an example from one of your past experiences when someone else got something you wanted and how you responded at the time. Knowing what you know today, how would you respond now?

....

....

....

....

....

....

....

....

....

....

....

Just as God opens doors that no person can shut, God closes doors that no person can open. Don't lose your peace because something bucked you off. If it's supposed to be yours, you can rest assured that nobody else will get it.

13. Read 1 Samuel 16:1–13. What does the statement "The oil that belongs to you cannot go to other people" mean? What does that say about times when people try to write you off?

....

....

....

....

....

....

14. The Scripture says, "No eye has seen, no ear has heard, and no mind has imagined what God has prepared for those who love him" (1 Cor. 2:9 NLT). Explain what that means when others see how God has already set you up for blessings.

> *If you've seen it, heard it, or imagined it, that's not what this is talking about.*

....

....

....

....

....

15. What powerful principle on the favor of God is reflected through the young lady who was instrumental in bringing a Night of Hope to the New York Yankee baseball stadium? What assurance does this give you about your future?

....

....

....

....

....

Sometimes there's a blessing already set up, but people will try to talk you out of it. But God didn't put the dream in them; He put the dream in you. They can't see what you see. They're looking at it in the ordinary, the natural, but God wouldn't have given you the dream, He wouldn't have put the promise in you, if He had not already set up how to bring it to pass.

16. Describe a time in your life when someone tried to talk you out of something that God put on your heart. Did you stay in faith and see it come to pass?

....

....

....

....

....

....

....

....

....

....

....

....

....

....

17. Read Matthew 6:33. What is the key to receiving the blessings God has already set up for you?

....

....

....

....

18. Read Isaiah 65:24. Describe how this promise from God was shown as true in Joseph's life when he was about to be left to die in a pit.

....

....

....

....

....

19. What does the story of the crushed car that was halfway off the high bridge graphically tell you about God's ability to set up blessings?

....

....

....

....

....

20. Based upon what you have learned in this chapter, take a moment and reflect on how you can start living every day with the confidence that everything you need to fulfill your destiny is already lined up.

> *God knows what you need, when you need it, and how to get it to you.*

....

....

....

....

....

....

....

Take Your Seat

In the Old Testament, the priests had to go into the temple at certain times of the year and make sacrifices for the people's sins. That's how they received forgiveness. It was all based around work. There were no chairs in the tabernacle, because there was no reason for seats. The priests couldn't sit down. They lived under the constant pressure that their work was never done. Another sacrifice was always required. But when Jesus was crucified, He said on the cross, "It is finished." He was talking about the old way of having to constantly work for God's goodness. The Scripture says, "He sat down at the right hand of the Father." Jesus' sitting is a picture of rest. Under the Old Covenant, the priests were constantly working, trying to cover the sins, trying to be good enough, trying to make things happen. Under the New Covenant, Jesus is sitting and resting.

Here's the beauty of it. The apostle Paul said in the book of Ephesians, "We are seated with Christ in the heavenly places." There is a seat of rest that belongs to you. You don't have to go through life wrought up inside, worried about your finances, trying to make a family member do what's right, or frustrated because a dream hasn't come to pass. Do yourself a favor. Take your seat. Enter into this rest. When you live seated, you're in peace.

You may have problems, but you know God is fighting your battles. People may have done you wrong, but you're not trying to pay them back because you know that God is your vindicator. He'll make your wrongs right. When you're struggling with an illness, and the medical report doesn't look good, you could go around upset and worried, but instead you stay seated. You know God has you in the palms of His hands. You know the number of your days, He will fulfill.

David said, "Though I am surrounded by trouble, my heart will know no fear, for the Lord will bring me safely through." He was saying, "Even though everything has come against me, and I should be worried and upset, I know a secret: The battle is not mine; the battle is the Lord's. So I'm going to take my seat." When you try to make everything happen in your own strength, you have to pay people back, fix all the problems, and live worried about a child. When you stand up, God steps back. As long as you're working, He'll rest. But when you sit down, God will stand up, so to speak. He'll go to work. That's why He told the Israelites again and again, "Be still, and you will see the deliverance of the Lord." He was saying, "Take your seat. I've got this. I'm bigger than what you're facing."

This doesn't mean that we don't do anything and just sit back passively all day long. We should be responsible. We have to pray, believe, and dream. But we do it from a place of rest. You can work hard with a rest inside, knowing that you're doing your best and God will get you to where you're supposed to be. You're not working hard but frustrated, thinking, *When am I going to get good breaks? Why hasn't this changed? Everybody's passing me up.* Well, take your seat. Work from a place of rest, knowing that God's favor is on your life, that He's breathing in your direction, that goodness and mercy are chasing you down.

Inner Rest

Inner rest is just as important as outer rest. Your physical body may rest, but if your mind never rests, if you live wrought up inside, fighting everything you don't like, that's going to wear you out. Even things you should stand against—an addiction, a sickness, a dysfunction—if you're always in fight mode, under pressure, constantly working and thinking, *I've got to change this*, it's going to drain your joy and your energy. You're living under the Old Covenant, under works. You're saying, "If I can work hard enough . . . if I can make myself change . . . if I can make this problem go away . . ." Your heart is right, but your approach is wrong. Why don't you approach it from a place of rest? "God, I can't change this on my own. I need Your help. I'm going to be my best. And I know that You're the Potter and I'm the clay. In Your time and in Your way, You will help me change." Instead of doing, doing, doing, the right attitude is *done, done, done.* It is finished. God has already defeated every enemy. He's already planned out your days for good. Now take your seat and live from a place of rest, a place of peace, a place of trust.

When I first started ministering, I would get so nervous. I knew I was supposed to step up and pastor the church after my father passed, but I dreaded getting up in front of people. All through the week I had to fight these thoughts: *What if I don't know what to say?*

What if nobody comes? What if people don't listen to me? When I would finish my last message on Sunday morning, for about thirty minutes I would be so relieved and so grateful. But then I would start thinking about the next week. *What am I going to say next Sunday? What if I can't come up with anything?* After about six months, I thought, *I am not living like this anymore. I'm going to take my seat.* If I had not made that decision, I wouldn't have made it to my fortieth birthday.

You weren't created to carry those heavy burdens, to be weighted down with worry, stress, and frustration. This is the reason some people have health issues. This is why they can't sleep at night, have digestive problems and high blood pressure. It's because there's no inner rest. They haven't learned how to take their seat. They're constantly worried about their child, trying to figure everything out, frustrated because it's taking so long. The psalmist says, "Be still and know that He is God." This infers that if you're not still, if you're not seated, you won't really know that He is God. You won't see His favor, His goodness, and His blessings as you should.

When things come against you, as they did me, it's easy to let your mind constantly play all the what-ifs. *What if it doesn't work out? What if the report isn't good? What if they don't change?* Remember, when you're working, God is resting. If you start resting, turning that over to God, then He'll start working. He sees what's happening. He knows how big the challenge is. He knows who did you wrong. The good news is, He already has the solution. He's not only going to bring you out, He's going to make the enemy pay and bring you out better than you were before. Now do your part and take your seat. Quit trying to figure everything out. There are no logical solutions to some situations. In one sense you have to turn your mind off. The Scripture says, "Lean not to your own understanding." It's okay to say, "God, I don't see how this can work out. I don't see a way." But don't stop there. Follow it up with, "But I know You have a way. I know this is not a surprise to You. You had the solution before I had the problem, so I'm not going to worry. I'm going to live from a place of peace."

Labor to Rest

David says, "God will make your enemies your footstool." A footstool is something you put your feet upon when you're sitting. It's another picture of rest. God could have said He would make our enemies like grass, so we could walk on them, or like sand, so it's soft. God used footstools to remind us to stay at rest. When you face challenges, things you don't understand, things that are not fair, one of the first things you need to do is put your feet up. Come back to a place of peace. You have to do this by faith, because every voice will tell you why it's not going to work out. *You're not going to get well. You saw the diagnosis. Your family will never be restored. There's too much strife.* That's the enemy trying to deceive you into standing up. He'll do everything he can to keep you from staying seated. He knows that when you're seated, when you're in peace, trusting God, he doesn't have a chance. When you live from a place of rest, all the forces of darkness cannot stop you. God has the final say. It may have been meant for your harm, but God is going to turn it into a footstool and not just a place of rest. Instead of it being a stumbling block to stop you, it's going to become a stepping-stone to take you to the next level.

It says in the book of Hebrews, "Labor to enter into the rest of God." That sounds like a contradiction: labor to rest. But God used the word *labor* because He knew it's going to take work to stay seated. It's easy to stand up. It's easy to be offended and try to pay people back. It's easy to live worried and discouraged by problems. That's why it says, "Labor to enter His rest." It's going to take effort. This is one of the few times that God tells us to work. It doesn't say, "Work to straighten out your neighbor. Work to make the problem go away." He says, "Work to stay seated."

Perhaps you're trying to break an addiction. Yes, you have to be disciplined. You have to be determined. But if there's a war going on inside, where you're upset with yourself, frustrated because you're not further along, or trying to force it to happen in your own strength, you're not tapping into the grace that's available today. You're like that Old Testament priest who had to make sacrifices again and again. No, you're under the New Covenant. Christ defeated every enemy, and the sacrificial price has already been paid, once and for all. You are not working to get the victory; you are working from the victory. When you know you've already won, there's a rest. You don't live worried. You don't lose sleep at night. You know the outcome. God says, "He always causes you to triumph." It may not turn out the way you thought or on your timetable, but God's ways are better than our ways. This is what trust is all about. What I'm saying is, when you live from a place of peace, you'll not only enjoy your life more, but God will make things happen that you couldn't make happen.

Put Up Some Boundaries

My parents started Lakewood in 1959 with ninety people. For about thirteen years, the church didn't really grow. They had less than two hundred people. My father had much bigger things in his heart. At seventeen years of age, he knew that one day he was going to pastor a church with thousands, but he wasn't seeing any of that. His friends would come by and say, "John, what are you doing out here still pastoring this little church?" They meant well, but sometimes your friends can be discouraging. They were saying, "John, why don't you stand up? Why don't you make something happen? Why don't you do it in your own strength?" My father's attitude was, *I'm going to keep doing what I know God wants me to do. I'm not going to be frustrated because the church is not growing. I'm not going to slack off because it hasn't turned out my way. I'm going to keep my seat.* He lived from this place of rest, knowing that God is in control, that God is keeping the records.

There are tests we have to pass. One of them is being faithful when nothing is changing, doing the right thing when it's not growing. It's easy to get frustrated and say, "God, I've got bigger things in me. Why isn't it changing?" No, keep your seat. God is watching you. He sees your faithfulness. He sees you doing the right thing when it's hard. At the appointed time, in your due season, God is going to catapult you further ahead than you can imagine. You are not falling behind; you are being prepared. God is getting you ready. Everything you went through deposited something inside. The delays made you stronger. The fact that you are not as far along as you would like was ordained by God. Perhaps you've had people who didn't support you or who walked away. You could have become bitter, but instead you stayed seated. You kept your peace. Now get ready. Your time is coming. God has something bigger than you think, more rewarding than you can imagine. He's going to exceed your expectations.

That's what happened to my father. He ended up pastoring a church with thousands and thousands. But sometimes the reason we're frustrated is we're trying to change things that only God can change. You can't make people do what's right. You can pray for them and encourage them, but they have their own free will. Don't let them steal your joy. You are not responsible for other people's happiness. You cannot keep everyone in your life happy. You are responsible for your own happiness. I don't mean that you should live selfishly, but sometimes we take on a false sense of responsibility. We think we have to keep all our neighbors happy, all our coworkers happy, all our friends happy, and all our family happy. I've learned that some people don't want to be happy. They just want your attention. They want you to cater to them and come running every time they call. If you don't, they'll try to make you feel guilty for not meeting all their demands. What they really want is to control you. Don't fall into that trap. Be nice. Be kind. But don't be a doormat. You have a destiny to fulfill. You have an assignment. It's easy to let people cause you to stand up, to lose your peace, and to live frustrated. No, sit back down. Stay at rest.

I had to learn this lesson because I always felt responsible for keeping everyone around me happy. It was easy when I was young and only had a few friends and family members. But as I got older and had more family, more friends, cousins, relatives, colleagues, and neighbors, I ended up spending half my time putting out fires. I had to calm one person down, cheer another one up, and run over to someone else so they wouldn't be offended. One day I finally realized I couldn't become who I'm created to be if I kept trying to please everybody around me. I had to draw the line in the sand and say, "I'm sitting down. I'm staying in peace. I'm not going to let people who won't take responsibility for their own happiness make me feel guilty and control me." I will be kind and go the extra mile, but some people are high maintenance. They will drain all the life, all the energy, and all the goodwill out of you if you allow them. They are not being disciplined to manage their own life and emotions, and they expect you to keep them fixed.

You cannot fulfill your destiny and accomplish your assignment unless you put up some boundaries. You cannot let people pull you out of rest, make you feel guilty, and get you upset, as though you have to keep them happy. That is a codependent relationship. If they can't be happy without you, that's not healthy. Be nice, but be firm. You have to labor to enter into this rest. God wouldn't have said "labor" if it wasn't going to be uncomfortable at times. I know you don't want to hurt people's feelings, but you are not doing them a favor by catering to them. You are enabling their dysfunction, and that's keeping you from moving forward. You have to set some boundaries. You can't come running every time they call. You shouldn't change your plans and not spend time with your family to go help them for the four hundredth time this month. Some people are alarmists. Every time they call, it's a major crisis, a major emergency, and it has to be dealt with right then. You have enough drama in your own life. You don't need somebody else's drama.

Don't Get Pulled Out of Rest

Years ago, I had a friend from high school with whom I played basketball. He's a fine young man, and I enjoyed being around him, but he started becoming overly dependent on me. I had to call him and tell him what all our friends were doing. I always had to go pick him up. I felt pressured. I was young and didn't know any better. I just did it. Later, he got married, and I got married, and I didn't have the time I'd had before. He couldn't understand that, and he would get upset. I tried to keep him happy. I'd go see him. "Let's go play basketball. Let's go hang out." But it was never enough. He'd call again and get upset if I couldn't do what he wanted. It got to the point where when I saw his name on my phone, I didn't want to answer it. I felt guilty, so I would answer. Then he'd tell me all the reasons why I wasn't being a good friend.

One day I finally learned what I'm telling you. I am not responsible to keep everyone around me happy. I was nice, but I stopped answering his calls. The surprising thing was,

I didn't feel guilty. I felt good about it. I knew he was pulling me out of rest. When some people are in your life, you cannot stay seated. If you don't make an adjustment, you'll be frustrated for the next twenty years. Be respectful, but put up some boundaries. "Well, Joel, what if they get upset? What if they don't want to be my friend?" Say, "Thank You, Jesus." They did you a favor!

Here's the bottom line: When you get to Heaven, you are not going to answer to people about what you did with your life, how you spent your time, and how you used your gifts. You're going to answer to God. Your destiny is too important to let people control you. There are a lot of things in life that we can't change. We can't make people do what's right. We can't make ourselves get well necessarily. We can't make a dream come to pass. But we can change our approach. We can choose to not let these things upset us. We can make a decision to take our seat. When somebody cuts you off in traffic, it's tempting to stand up. It's tempting to get upset, to try to cut them off, and to blow your horn, but they're already in the next lane speeding away. You might as well sit back down. Don't let a stranger pull you out of rest. It's not hurting them, but it's souring your day.

A lot of these things are simply tests. Are we going to keep letting the same things upset us? Let the same people get on our nerves? Let the same delays sour our life? My message is very simple: Stay seated. This is a freeing way to live. When you know that God is in control, that nothing can happen without His permission, and that He is directing your steps, it takes the pressure off. You can live calm, in peace, not fighting everything you don't like. You have a disappointment, perhaps the medical report is not good, but you say, "I'm not going to worry. I'm staying seated. God is my healer." If you have a setback in your finances or you lose a big client, every voice will say, "Be worried. Be upset. That's not fair." But if you listen closely, you'll hear the still small voice saying, "Stay seated. God's working behind the scenes. Payback is coming. Abundance is on the way." I wonder how much more we'd enjoy life if we learned to live from this place of rest.

Rise above the Challenge

In the Scripture, it compares the life of a believer to an eagle. It's interesting how an eagle handles some challenges. A crow is one of the eagle's biggest pests. When the eagle is flying low, the crow will come up right behind it and pester it, doing things to annoy it. Even though the eagle is much bigger, it can't turn as fast as the crow. So instead of fighting the crow, getting upset, and trying to defend itself, the eagle will simply stretch out its seven-foot wingspan, catch the wind, and rise higher and higher. An eagle can fly to heights of ten thousand feet. The crow normally does not fly over three hundred feet high and will just fall away.

In the same way, we all have some crows in our life. We have some chickens and turkeys too. We have people who want to irritate us, to get on our nerves, and do things to try to bait us into conflict. It's easy to get upset and try to straighten every crow out. But remember that you're an eagle. You can go higher. You can fly where the crows won't go.

But if you stay down at their level and try to straighten out every crow and get involved in conflicts that don't matter, that will keep you from your destiny. The crows, the chickens, and the turkeys are simply distractions.

When an eagle faces a storm, when there's bad weather in its path, it doesn't put down its head and try to force its way through it. It doesn't fight the winds or fight the rain and thunder. It catches the thermal winds and rises higher until it's above all the turmoil. Like the eagle, we all face storms. We all have difficulties. The key is to rise above all the turmoil. You don't have to fight your way through it. Don't let it get inside. Remain at rest. Stay seated, and God will fight your battles. Too often we're fighting when we should be resting. We're standing when we should be sitting. And, yes, we have to stand strong. I'm talking about in your spirit. Even when it's stormy all around you, when things are happening that you don't understand, you need to have a rest, knowing that God is still on the throne, that He is bigger than anything you're facing. When you're an eagle, when you've learned to rise above the challenges, you'll be at peace when you could be upset. You'll have a smile when you could be discouraged. You're showing God that you trust Him. You're taking your seat.

Sometimes after a long day, I'll be standing in our family kitchen talking to Victoria and our children. We can talk for a long time, but at some point I'll tell them, "I have to go get off my feet." I know when I'm done, when I need to sit down and relax. Maybe today you need to get off your feet. You're living worried about your health, stressed over your finances, upset because your child still hasn't changed. Why don't you come back to a place of peace? God has it all figured out. Those enemies and obstacles you're concerned about are not going to stop you. They're going to become a footstool. Instead of laboring to try and fix everything, I'm asking you to labor to enter this rest. You weren't created to carry the heavy burdens. There is a seat of rest that has your name on it. You may have been standing for a long time, but God is saying, "Take your seat." Live from a place of rest. Work hard. Do your best. But inside, stay in peace. If you do this, you're not only going to enjoy life more, but God is going to bring dreams to pass, turn around problems, and restore health to you. You're going to see the life of victory that belongs to you.

Take Your Seat

In the Old Testament, the priests had to go into the temple at certain times of the year and make sacrifices for the people's sins. That's how they received forgiveness. It was all based around work. There were no chairs in the tabernacle, because there was no reason for seats. The priests couldn't sit down. They lived under the constant pressure that their work was never done. Another sacrifice was always required.

1. Read John 19:30 and Hebrews 10:12. Contrast the work of the Old Testament priests to the position of Jesus under the New Covenant.

    ....

    ....

    ....

    ....

    ....

2. The apostle Paul says, "God raised us up with Christ and seated us with him in the heavenly realms in Christ Jesus" (Eph. 2:6 NIV). What does it mean to be seated with Christ? Have you recognized this is true in your life? In what ways do you, and in what ways have you not?

    ....

    ....

    ....

    ....

    ....

3. The Scripture says, "Though I am surrounded by troubles, you will bring me safely through them…. Your power will save me" (Ps. 138:7 TLB). What was David saying? What happens when you try to make everything happen in your own strength? How have you found this principle to be true in your life?

....

....

....

"Be still, and you will see the deliverance of the Lord."

....

....

....

....

....

....

....

....

4. What is the difference between working in your own strength, working from a place of rest, and being passive about your life?

....

....

....

....

....

....

....

....

Inner rest is just as important as outer rest. Your physical body may rest, but if your mind never rests, if you live wrought up inside, fighting everything you don't like, that's going to wear you out. It's going to drain your joy and your energy.

5. Name an area of your life that you are working and working to change but it's not working. What new attitude do you need to have? Write a prayer that you can say each morning that reflects the prayer in Isaiah 64:8.

    ....

    ....

    ....

    ....

    ....

    ....

    ....

    ....

    ....

6. Have you noticed health issues in your life that are related to the worry, stress, and frustrations you carry? What are they, and what change in your thinking and attitude will help you improve in this area?

    ....

    ....

    ....

    ....

    ....

    ....

    ....

7. When things come against you, it's easy to let your mind constantly play all the what-ifs. What is coming against you today, and what are the what-ifs that want to play in your mind? What truth about God can you use to answer those what-ifs?

> *You weren't created to carry around heavy burdens of worry and stress.*

....

....

....

....

....

....

....

....

8. Write out Proverbs 3:5 and take some time to memorize this powerful verse of Scripture. Describe an issue in your life where you need to apply this verse, and write a statement that declares you are going to live from a place of peace.

....

....

....

....

....

....

....

....

....

....

....

9. In Psalm 110, David says, "God will make your enemies your footstool." When you face a challenge, what does that tell you is one of the first things you need to do? What is the enemy's favorite tactic of getting you to stand up?

....

....

....

....

....

....

....

....

10. The Scripture says, "Let us labor therefore to enter into that rest" (Heb. 4:11 KJV). Explain how that statement is not a contradiction.

....

....

....

....

....

11. Sometimes we feel as though there's a war going on inside to overcome an issue, but we can't beat it. How does being under the New Covenant of grace change that?

....

....

....

....

....

....

....

12. When something is not working out as you thought or changing as you desire, what is one of the tests you need to pass? What does God have in store for you?

....

....

....

....

....

....

13. Sometimes the reason we're frustrated is we're trying to change things that only God can change. How is that especially true when it comes to dealing with other people?

> *Live from a place of rest, knowing God is in control.*

....

....

....

....

....

14. To what level do you see yourself being a people pleaser? Describe how you respond when other people demand your attention and want you to cater to them.

....

....

....

....

....

....

....

15. You cannot fulfill your destiny and accomplish your assignment unless you put up some boundaries. What are some boundaries that you need to put up in your relationships? How can you do that respectfully and kindly and yet firmly?

....
....
....
....
....
....
....

16. People try to control us in many ways. What is the bottom line that you need to realize about how you live your life?

....
....
....
....
....

17. How can you keep from letting the same things upset you? Write down an example that you need to correct now.

....
....
....
....
....

18. What valuable lesson can you learn from the way an eagle deals with a pesky crow?

....

....

....

....

....

....

19. When you face one of life storms, how can you be like an eagle and not fight it?

....

....

....

....

....

....

20. How do you feel, knowing that you can take your seat and live from a place of rest? Spend some time giving thanks to the Lord and share with Him how this blesses you.

Work hard.
Do your best.
But inside,
stay in peace.

....

....

....

....

....

....

Stay connected, be blessed.

Get more from Joel & Victoria Osteen

It's time to step into the life of victory and favor that God has planned for you! Featuring new messages from Joel & Victoria Osteen, their free daily devotional and inspiring articles, hope is always at your fingertips with the free Joel Osteen app and online at JoelOsteen.com.

Get the app and visit us today at JoelOsteen.com.

The Rewards of Integrity

In this message, Joel reminds us about the power of a life lived with integrity. Integrity is the foundation that a successful life is built on. God is looking for people who are willi...

PLAY